D1551708

APACHE WOMEN WARRIORS

APACHE WOMEN WARRIORS

Kimberly Moore Buchanan

Texas
Western
Press

The University of Texas at El Paso

Southwestern Studies Series No. 79

Library of Congress Catalog Card No. 86-050099

First Edition
3rd Printing 1996
ISBN 0-87404-154-6 (paper)
ISBN 0-87404-157-0 (cloth)

∞ Texas Western Press books are printed on acid free paper.

CONTENTS

INTRODUCTION

The Apache are a people who have been explored by many writers, and although there is an abundance of material dealing with them, many voids and misconceptions still persist. One neglected area is the study of the alternative roles of women. Usually native American women are regarded and portrayed as mere supporting characters, but among many tribes were those who defied the erroneous stereotype of the drudging squaw. Many Apache wives accompanied their husbands on raiding and warring parties and, on the whole, exercised a tremendous amount of freedom and power. An unmarried woman also was known to have distinguished herself as a warrior in her own right.

This study explores accounts of Apache wives and other native American women who encompassed alternative gender roles. Special attention is given to one exceptional Warm Springs Apache woman known as Lozen, "The Woman Warrior." She is said to have been an unmarried sister of the noted Warm Springs chief Victorio, after whose death she joined Geronimo's band. Her prowess as a warrior and her extraordinary supernatural ability to locate the enemy earned her a legendary status among her people.

As scholars of native American history are aware, the paucity of written sources is an overriding research problem. As a result, much of the work done in this field draws heavily on oral tradition. My research is no exception. I gratefully acknowledge the invaluable assistance of Eve Ball, who shared her extraordinary oral history research with me. She spent many years conducting interviews with the Chiricahua and Mescalero Apaches living on the Mescalero Reservation near Ruidoso, New Mexico. These interviews are incorporated into two of her most outstanding books, *In the Days of Victorio: Recollections of a Warm Springs Apache* narrated by James Kawaykla and *Indeh: An Apache Odyssey*. A remarkable historian, she brought to public attention many previously unknown stories of the Apache people.

I also want to acknowledge the guidance of Dr. John R. Wunder, who channeled my interests in native American history. My husband Dennis and parents, Elvin R. and Rildabeth Moore, receive my loving gratitude.

CHAPTER ONE

THE APACHE: SURVIVORS

WHAT IS LIFE IF WE ARE IMPRISONED LIKE CATTLE IN A CORRAL?
WE HAVE BEEN A WILD, FREE PEOPLE, FREE TO COME AND GO AS
WE WISHED. HOW CAN WE BE CAGED?

Victorio[1]

The Apache, or Indeh as they refer to themselves, have become legendary American figures. In popular literature and other media they are characteristically portrayed as murdering savages. While their history was marred by violent and tragic encounters with Spanish, Mexican, and Anglo-American settlers and military forces, the perpetrated violence was not the sole result of Apache savagery as the public has been led to believe. Fortunately, in the last twenty years, a more objective picture of the Apaches has emerged. They were a diverse society with worthy and interesting cultural traditions. Among their outstanding qualities was the ability to survive in the face of great adversity. They dominated a great portion of the Southwest for approximately three hundred years and resisted persistent subjugation attempts until 1886. Their intense struggle is a tribute to their fierce loyalty to remain a free and proud people. The Apaches worked together to retain their traditional lifestyle and, in a large measure, succeeded in achieving this goal. Apache men are not the only individuals to be credited in this struggle for survival. Apache women deserve recognition also. Survival was a goal for all Apaches — male or female, adult or child.

The Apache were strong believers in supernatural power and religious spirits. They explained their origin in a creation legend comparable to those found in other societies. It centered on Ussen (or Yusn), the Apache Creator of Life, and four power-spirits:

> When it came time to form the earth, Yusn told four power-spirits to do it for him. They were Black Water, Black Metal, Black Wind and Black Thunder. Together they fashioned the earth, but when they were finished they saw it was no good. It was cold and dead. To make it live, Black Water gave it blood by causing the rivers to flow. Black Metal gave it a skeleton of hills and mountains. This way it was strong. Black Wind breathed life into the earth by causing the wind to blow. The earth was there in the universe, but it was cold, so Black Thunder clothed the earth in trees and grass. This way it was made warm.[2]

The legend illustrated the Apaches' great respect for religion and nature. Like all other native Americans, they were lovers of the land.

The Apaches were members of the Athapaskan language group. The starting point for their migration into the Southwest is believed to be the forested valleys between the Mackenzie and Yukon rivers in the Canadian Northwest.[3] Several reasons are hypothesized for this southward migration. The most accepted theories are that the Apaches moved as a result of pressure from other societies or followed migrating herds of bison into the Plains area.[4] Their southward migration probably occurred some time after A.D. 1000, following the eastern edge of the Rocky Mountains.[5]

Historians, linguists, and other scholars place the arrival of the Athapaskans in the Southwest sometime between 1400 and 1600. Pedro de Castañeda, chronicler of the 1540-42 expedition of Francisco Vásquez de Coronado, reported that the Pueblo Indians told of a group of people they called the Teyas who first appeared in the region around 1524.[6] Coronado's expedition encountered the Teyas and another group, the Querechos, in 1541. Castañeda described both in his journal: "They go about like nomads with their tents and packs of dogs harnessed with little pads, pack-saddles and girths. . . ."[7] Coronado commented on their economical use of every part of the bison. He noted that they not only ate the meat, but also utilized the skin, sinews, bones, bladder, and dung.[8] These descriptions lead scholars to surmise that the Teyas and Querechos were Athapaskan peoples.[9]

While the Athapaskans were relative latecomers to the Plains, they quickly dispersed and settled in the vast area that was to become the central United States. The Apachean group of the southern Athapaskans eventually came to occupy and claim an area dubbed the "Gran Apachería" by the Spaniards. This region included all of New Mexico and parts of Texas, Colorado, Kansas, Arizona, and northern Mexico, in scope approximately seven hundred by six hundred miles.[10] Written documents do not verify the existence of native Americans in any substantial number in this specific area until the 1600s. Reports from seventeenth-century Spanish expeditions referred to large numbers of nomadic peoples on the southern Plains. The word Apache is first found in the records of the Juan de Oñate expedition into the northern provinces of New Spain in 1598.[11]

Linguistically, the southern Athapaskans were divided into eastern and western groups. These two were divided further into separate nations according to territorial, cultural, and linguistic differences. The Jicarilla, Lipan, and Kiowa-Apache bands formed the eastern group, with the Navajo, Mescalero, Western, and Chiricahua composing the western faction.[12] The Apacheans may have arrived in the Southwest as a more or less homogeneous group, but due to varying pressures, the bands separated and drifted apart.[13]

During the seventeenth century, before extensive white contact, each Apachean group occupied certain regions with identifiable boundaries. The Mescaleros controlled an area in present-day southeastern New Mexico and northern Mexico, roughly bounded by the Rio Grande on the west and the Pecos River on the east. The Lipans occupied a region in central Texas, and in the early 1800s migrated to a small area in northern New Mexico. The Kiowa-Apache first settled in a small area where the present-day states of Wyoming, South Dakota, and Nebraska meet; they later migrated to southern Colorado along the Arkansas River. The Navajo settled in upper western New Mexico, eastern Arizona, and a small portion of southeastern Utah. The Western Apache patrolled a large area of east central Arizona. The Chiricahua ruled a vast area of southeastern Arizona, southwestern New Mexico, and northern Mexico.

The Chiricahua band will be the main focus of this study. Its members were divided into central, southern, and eastern bands, whose prominent leaders included Mangas Colorado, Del Gadito, Cochise, and Victorio. James Kawaykla, a Warm Springs Apache, said the tribe was more correctly divided into four groups:

1. The true Chiricahua, which were the groups led by Cochise and Chihuahua.
2. The Warm Springs, the Chihenne, or "red people," a name referring to a band of red clay drawn across the warriors' faces.
3. Nednhi, whose stronghold was in the Sierra Madre mountain range of Mexico; they were led by Juh.
4. Bedonkohes; Geronimo was their medicine man and their territory was around the headwaters of the Gila River.[14]

The Chiricahua were bitter foes of the Spanish, Comanche, and Mexicans from the sixteenth to eighteenth centuries. This unfortunate enmity was followed by an even more hostile American and Chiricahua experience. The Chiricahua were adamant about retaining control of their homelands, and the United States government was equally resolved to add these lands to its growing domain. The confrontation reached a peak after the Mexican-American War, and was followed by forty years of unsuccessful diplomatic negotiations and violence.

Teodoro de Croix, commander general of the Interior Provinces of New Spain from 1776 to 1783, reported that the war with the Apaches generally began in 1748 in Nueva Vizcaya. The *Rudo Ensayo*, a 1763 work by an unknown Jesuit priest, said of the Apache threat in Sonora, another province:

> Indeed it is a mercy of God that they [the Apaches] are themselves ignorant of their own strength, were they united against us, for there is not a place in the Province which could be held against their entire force, and in less than a year they could ruin it completely.[15]

The Apaches posed such a threat to Spanish settlers that it became common practice for the Spanish government to sell Apaches as slaves.[16]

The Apache hostilities reached such an extreme in the late sixteenth century that the Spanish created a special bureaucracy to deal with the problem. In 1776 Spanish officials established a military institution known as the Commandancy General of the Interior Provinces whose major function was to protect the provinces from Indian attack. Due to

Three divisions of the Chiricahua Apaches (Adapted from Thomas E. Mails, *The People Called Apache*).

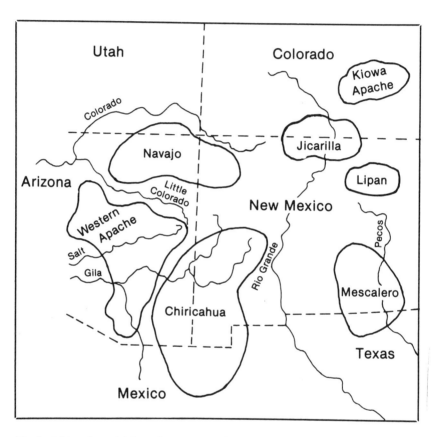

Territorial locations of Athapaskan groups (Adapted from Thomas E. Mails, *The People Called Apache*).

mismanagement, the system failed.[17] By 1835 most Spanish settlers in northern Sonora had abandoned their homes because of continued Apache raiding. Those who remained were advocates of a governmental policy called a "war of extermination" with the payment of money for Apache scalps.[18] One hundred pesos were paid for an adult male scalp, fifty for that of a woman, and twenty-five for a child's.[19] As further incentive, on 25 May 1849 the province of Chihuahua enacted the Fifth Law which provided a reward of 200 pesos for each warrior killed, 250 for each taken prisoner, and 150 for a female captive or Indian child, with a scalp as acceptable proof of a killing.[20] This legalized murder was profitable for Mexican citizens; in 1849 alone some 17,869 pesos were paid for Apache scalps.[21] Not surprisingly, the Apaches remembered this barbarous practice, and they always held a bitter resentment against the Mexican government and citizens.

Initial encounters between the Chiricahua and the United States military forces were relatively peaceful. Troops led by Brigadier General Stephen Watts Kearny met a band of the Warm Springs Apaches in 1846. First Lieutenant William Helmsley Emory of the topographical engineers recorded the encounter in his journal:

> A large number of Indians had collected about us, all differently dressed, and some in the most fantastical style. The Mexican dress and saddles predominated, showing where they had chiefly made up their wardrobe. . . . The light and graceful manner in which they mounted and dismounted, always on the right side, was the admiration of all. The children are on horseback from infancy.[22]

This apparently innocent and pleasant meeting did not foreshadow the future violence that would occur between these two groups.

The treaty ending the Mexican-American War gave control of the Chiricahua homelands to the United States, resulting in intensified Chiricahua and American contact. The Chiricahua were skilled raiders whose resolve to survive and retain their homeland at any cost set the stage for controversy. In 1852 John Russell Bartlett, a member of the United States Boundary Commission, wrote this account of Chiricahua activity in the southwestern United States and northern Mexico:

> The Copper Mine Apaches have been among the boldest of these depredators, and the names of their chiefs, Mangas Colorado, Del Gadito, Coleto Amarillo, and Ponce have

> struck terror among the people of Sonora, Chihuahua and those portions of New Mexico and Texas which border on the Rio Grande.[23]

Recognizing that a confrontation of some sort was inevitable, Bartlett proposed that the establishment of an Indian agent for each Chiricahua band might be the remedy to the situation.[24] This suggestion set the governmental wheels in motion.

United States officials decided to deal with the Apaches just as they had initially dealt with all other native American peoples — by negotiating treaties. Among the first between the Warm Springs Apaches and the United States was that of 1852, setting standards of behavior in the Southwest. The treaty consisted of eleven articles, with Article 2 summarizing the basic intent of the document:

> From and after the signing of this Treaty hostilities between the contracting parties shall forever cease, and perpetual peace and amity shall forever exist between said Indians and the Government and people of the United States.[25]

Other articles provided for the recognized jurisdiction of the United States; punishment of United States citizens who committed crimes against the Apaches; free and safe passage, as well as honest and humane treatment, of United States citizens crossing Apache territory; establishment of military posts and trading houses; and the cessation of Apache aggression in Mexico and surrender of Mexican captives. The agreement did not specifically account for the transferral of land rights from the Apaches to the United States government, but Article 9 covertly gave the United States broad authority over the territory:

> Relying confidently upon the justice and the liberality of the aforesaid government, and anxious to remove every possible cause that might disturb their peace and quiet it is agreed by the aforesaid Apaches that the government of the United States shall at its earliest convenience designate, settle, and adjust their territorial boundaries, and pass and execute in their territory such laws as may be deemed conducive to the prosperity and happiness of said Indians.[26]

Not surprisingly, this agreement was a failure. In the next twenty years relations progressively worsened and the government took other measures.

During the 1870s the Warm Springs bands were shuffled from one reservation to another. In 1870 Fort Apache, Arizona, was established to control the Navajo and Apache. The year 1871 was characterized by numerous Apache-American military confrontations; as a result, General George Crook organized four major Apache reservations, three in Arizona and one in New Mexico. The Warm Springs were initially sent to the Ojo Caliente in Arizona where an 1876 census showed that they numbered 916 men, women, and children.[27] Although unhappy with the restricting reservation life, they were relatively content because they had been allowed to stay in their homeland; however, they were distressed to learn of their planned relocation to the San Carlos Reservation in the desolate White Mountains of Arizona. Victorio's followers were assigned to the old Camp Goodwin on the San Carlos Reservation. Dan Thrapp, in *Victorio and the Mimbres Apaches*, described why this location was "an unfortunate choice":

> Malarial, barren, unattractive, with no good hunting grounds nearby but plenty of enemies among their [the Warm Springs] cousins, it was a ranchería for unhappiness. . . .[28]

On 1 September 1878, under the leadership of Victorio and Loco, approximately 310 members of the Warm Springs band fled from Camp Goodwin. On 29 September Victorio, with approximately 150 other Warm Springs Apaches, appeared at Wingate, Arizona, to surrender. General Philip H. Sheridan decided on 30 October that the 233 Warm Springs Apaches who had come in could return to their Ojo Caliente homeland.[29] On 22 July 1879 General William Sherman ordered the Ojo Caliente prisoners back to San Carlos. Victorio's band reacted violently to this order, rebelling against the American government and the military. They remained off the reservation and roamed southern New Mexico and Arizona and northern Mexico. They were credited with the deaths of more than two hundred New Mexican citizens, more than one hundred United States soldiers, and two hundred Mexicans between their first reservation outbreak and his death in 1881.[30] Victorio was killed in a battle with Mexican troops at Tres Castillos. Mexican soldiers bragged of killing the chief, while the Warm Springs people say he committed suicide with his own knife.[31]

After Victorio's death, Nana, a 73-year-old eccentric and charismatic leader, assumed control of the small number of Warm Springs survivors. He led his party on a series of raids to avenge the death of

Victorio. One account credited Nana and his warriors with the capture of two hundred horses while eluding fourteen hundred soldiers and civilians during the raids, which lasted for six weeks and covered a radius of one thousand miles.[32] Nana and his followers then drifted into northern Mexico where they accidentally encountered another small renegade Chiricahua band led by the famous Nednhi Apache medicine man Geronimo.[33] United, the two bands continued to escape their pursuers. Nana eventually left Geronimo's band, and with a small number of warriors led another devastating series of raids across New Mexico.[34]

In the 1880s Geronimo became the primary concern of the United States military. American military leaders feared that the Apaches on the reservation would see that Geronimo and his people were successfully retaining their freedom and would escape from the reservation to join them. Officers at the Fort Apache Reservation were convinced that the Apaches there would ". . .attempt to join Geronimo at the slightest provoction."[35] As a safeguard, all the Chiricahuas on the reservation were detained as prisoners of war pending resolution of the Geronimo troubles.

In September 1886, having been located by the military through the help of Apache scouts, Geronimo and members of his band met with Lieutenant Charles B. Gatewood to negotiate a surrender. Gatewood was acting under the direction of General Nelson E. Miles who was receiving direct orders from Washington, D.C. The Apaches initially negotiated with Gatewood and then officially surrendered to Miles whose promises to them during these talks were far from honorable. While Miles was promising Geronimo safe conduct, he was receiving orders from President Grover Cleveland and the War Department that read:

> I hope nothing will be done with Geronimo which will prevent our treating him as a prisoner of war, if we cannot hang him, which I would much prefer.[36]

Miles assured Geronimo that his people would be given a reservation with horses and wagons, while the War Department was ordering him to send the Apaches to Fort Marion in Florida to be retained as prisoners of war.[37] Unfortunately for the Apaches, Geronimo trusted the word of Miles; consequently, the band was shipped to Florida.

Under the official status of prisoners of war, the Apaches were sent to Florida by train. The men were left at Fort Pickens in Pensacola and the women and children were removed to Fort Marion in Saint Augustine.[38] The Chiricahuas, who had been living peacefully at Fort Apache, Arizona, were herded into corrals and barns, and then were sent to Florida to join Geronimo's band in compliance with the governmental aim of clearing Arizona of all Chiricahua Apaches. On 14 October 1886 Lieutenant C.P. Johnson of the Tenth Cavalry obtained the surrender of the last so-called hostile band of Chiricahuas and exiled these six adults and seven children to Florida as well.[39] At this time the total number of prisoners there was 498.[40] At last General Miles felt it safe to proclaim that the military had successfully cleared the ". . .territories of Arizona and New Mexico of the whole hostile element."[41]

The Chiricahua Apache were a remarkable people, proudly determined to maintain their nomadic lifestyle. In order to survive, they relied on everyone in the band to fulfill necessary roles. Men usually served as leaders and warriors, but Chiricahua women were also capable in these roles. Women were vital participants in the struggle for survival, with a combination of factors allowing them to enjoy independent lifestyles. They participated in the traditional male activities of hunting, raiding, and warring that were normally forbidden to their contemporary feminine counterparts in more established, stable, and populous societies. The Chiricahua quest for freedom transcended usual gender roles.

CHAPTER TWO

APACHE WOMEN: pROVIdERS ANd lEAdERS

MUCH HAS BEEN WRITTEN OF THE LOW REGARD IN WHICH IN-
DIAN WOMEN WERE HELD. AMONG MY PEOPLE THAT WAS NOT
TRUE. INSTEAD, THEY WERE RESPECTED, PROTECTED, AND
CHERISHED.

James Kawaykla[42]

In almost every known culture throughout history, gender has been
a major role determinant. Conditions varied greatly among the many
native North American tribes, but their women as individuals and as
groups often possessed a great deal of power and authority over their
own destinies.[43] Most native American tribes were in some way
centered around the female figure. They were either matrifocal, with
the mother role considered culturally and structurally central;
matrilineal, where the line of descent was traced through the mother;
matrilocal, where the husband lived with his wife's family after marriage; or a combination of these social structures. The Apaches were a
matrilocal tribe; as a result, women held a high position in the social
hierarchy.

The matrilocal predominance extended power to Apache females, as
well as imposing rigid obligations on males.[44] When a daughter married, she moved to a separate dwelling with her new husband. The
groom was bound to his wife's parents by strict cultural traditions and

practices.[45] Apache women were protected from unwanted male advances and had powerful influence in such matters as marriage, divorce, and residence.

Apache girls usually married at a young age, but not before the puberty ceremony that marked their first menstruation. By the time of a girl's ceremony, she had completed her domestic training and was prepared to be a wife and mother. An early marrying age also lessened the possibility of premarital sex, a practice strictly frowned upon by the Apaches. Most marriages were economic arrangements, although personal feelings were not totally disregarded. Separate bands always needed strong men; since the new husband joined his wife's band and brought marriage gifts with him, marriage was an economic asset for the bride's family. In *An Apache Life-Way* by Morris E. Opler, an Apache explained these arrangements:

> At marriage a man goes to the camp of the girl's parents to live. We do this because a woman is more valuable than a man. We do it to accommodate the woman. The son-in-law is considered a son and as one of the family. The in-laws depend a great deal on him. They depend on him for hunting and all kinds of work. He is almost a slave to them. Everything he gets on the hunt goes to them.[46]

Obviously, an Apache marriage favored the females. The groom was the one who made the major adjustments and sacrifices, while the bride and her family were the gracious recipients, allowed to remain in their familiar environment.

In addition to changing residence and providing for a new family, the groom also had to present a marriage gift to his bride and her family. The usual gift was a horse or a hide. The amount or size of the gift only represented the wealth of the groom, not the status of the bride. Its ultimate function was to serve as evidence of the groom's future economic support, cooperation, and loyalty toward his prospective in-laws.[47]

Being a mother and rearing healthy children were the traditional goals for a woman in most North American Indian societies. Women were valued for their roles as childbearers. Pregnant Apache women refrained from strenuous activities and were treated with consideration and respect. The Apaches were known for their great love of children. Both male and female children were equally desirable, with no preference as to the sex of the firstborn. Daughters were considered to be greater economic assets due to matrilocal practices.

The everyday lives of Apache women were strenuous and not extremely colorful, and their duties were central to their people's survival. In some Native American societies women accounted for as much as 80 percent of the labor needed in hunting and gathering the food supply.[48] Apache women probably accounted for a similar percentage of the work done in their bands, giving them a great deal of power. A wife maintained an active and close relationship with her family's food supply, and ultimately, its survival. Without a mother or female guardian, a family's very existence was threatened.

Food gathering was the major responsibility of Apache women. Food available near the camp was gathered by an individual woman or a small group of females; another group traveled to a more distant harvest area.[49] Hunting was the man's responsibility, but it was not unusual for the woman to hunt also. James Kawaykla recalled the various duties given to the women of his band:

> Mother killed deer and the women tanned the hides and made moccasins. They cut meat into thin strips, not across, but with the grain, and dried it. They made dresses from a bolt of calico cached in the cave. And they used the cooking pots left there. . . .[50]

The responsibility of providing food for the family made a woman the key provider.

In addition to the traditional tasks of food gathering and preparation, hide tanning and garment fashioning, shelter building, wood gathering, fire building, and child rearing, Apache girls were taught other skills. They were instructed in the medicinal values of plants and the nursing of minor ailments. A girl usually learned by observing her mother, grandmother, sister, or another older woman. Young girls also learned child-rearing techniques by observation. One of the first duties of an Apache girl was that of caring for her own younger brothers and sisters.[51]

Even though domestic chores were stressed, maturing Apache girls also were encouraged to develop their physical strength. They received the same basic training as boys, and all learned to be strong and vigorous. The girls were told to "rise early, run often, and shun no hard work."[52] All children needed to be able to reach safety quickly in case of an attack.[53] James Kawaykla told of the importance of children keeping their knives and emergency rations with them at all times. If the band was caught by a surprise attack and had to flee, each child would be equipped with the basic necessities for survival.[54] Another fundamental skill that was practiced daily by both boys and girls was horsemanship.[55] All children were taught to mount an unsaddled horse without assistance. Boys and girls also learned archery skills and often played in a realistic manner by pretending to hunt and stalk imaginary game with makeshift bows and arrows and spears.[56] There were stories of girls who rivaled the fastest boys in foot races, and many of the fastest girls were allowed to participate in rabbit hunts.[57]

As the children grew older, joint play was discouraged. They were gradually relegated to separate social spheres. Girls were allowed to cross over into the "male" sphere of activities quite often and without fear of ridicule, but boys did not dare be seen doing domestic chores.

In most Apache societies there were very few cultural domains closed to women. In other seventeenth- and eighteenth-century non-Indian societies, women did not have the same opportunities to hold positions of leadership and prestige. Apache women attended celebrations and ceremonies with the men and were able to obtain supernatural power on the same level as males.[58] Many of the supernatural beings that assumed important roles in native American religion and folklore were females. Almost all North American tribes had feminine mother dieties. Feminine qualities were almost always given to the earth, and in Apache ceremonies the earth was referred to as "Earth Mother."[59]

In Apache religion the supreme deity was Ussen (or Yusn) which meant Life-Giver. Ussen was given no particular gender. Ussen's contemporary was White Painted Woman, the mother of Child of the Waters, the dominant Apache culture hero.[60] Apache children grew up learning about these spirits. White Painted Woman was believed to have existed since the beginning of time. A very powerful and important deity, she personified the Apachean respect for females.

White Painted Woman also played the central role in the puberty ceremony, the most elaborate and celebrated Apache ritual which marked a girl's first menstruation. In virtually every native American culture, menstruation has been regarded as a mysterious and fearful phenomenon. In *The Curse: A Cultural History of Menstruation*, this prevailing fear is examined:

> Greater than his fear of death, dishonor, or dismemberment has been primitive man's respect for menstrual blood. The measures he has taken to avoid this mysterious substance have affected his mealtimes, his bedtimes, and his hunting season.[61]

To combat this fear, taboos were created. The taboos of menstruation were practices that prompted the isolation, whether physically, sexually, or psychologically, of the menstruating female from the rest of her village. These taboos were among the most inviolate of many societies.[62]

The Apaches respected the menstrual taboo, but they did not carry the isolation of the menstruating female to the extreme found in many other native American societies. Numerous tribes advocated and required the complete physical isolation of menstruating women and considered it extremely dangerous for anyone, especially a man, to even look at a woman experiencing her menstrual flow. An Apache girl was counseled by her mother, grandmother, or another female relative in preparation for her first menstrual period. She was told that "menstrual blood is dangerous to men."[63] An Apache boy would be warned that "contact with menstrual discharges will make his joints swell and ache."[64] As a result, men feared menstrual blood and abstained from intercourse with menstruating women. Apache men did not fear the female, but rather the menstrual blood itself. This distinction allowed Apache women to escape the complete physical isolation and ostracism that a large number of other native American females withstood.

Ironically, Apaches regarded menstruation in a highly positive manner also. The puberty ceremony was the focal point for Apache ritual, society, and economy, and it marked a young Apache maiden's entrance into womanhood. During the four-day and four-night ceremony, the girl was referred to as White Painted Woman, and her clothing duplicated the costume of the deity. Every Apache girl was expected to participate in the ceremony, and preparations began as soon as it became evident that a girl was approaching puberty. Although the ceremony was expensive for a girl's family, its importance was unquestioned. Tribal members believed that any girl who failed to go through the rite would not be healthy or have a long life.[65] This elaborate ceremony, especially designed to honor females, unequivocally demonstrated the immense power of women in Apache society.

An objective observation of Apache women showed individuals who exercised tremendous power and leadership potential. They were not passive wives completely subservient to every whim of their domineering husbands, as often portrayed in popular literature, but enjoyed considerable freedom both inside and outside the domestic sphere. They had essential functions in religious ideology, societal structure, tribal economics, ceremonial rituals, and in some cases, traditionally male pursuits. This high regard and respect for Apache females is instrumental in understanding why some women were able to pursue alternative lifestyles with such facility.

CHAPTER THREE

APACHE WIVES:
SUPPORTERS ANd fiGHTERS

"WHERE'S MOTHER?" I ASKED. "SHE RIDES WITH YOUR FATHER
AND NANA ON ANOTHER RAID."

James Kawaykla[66]

The Apaches relied on raiding as a primary means of existence, un-justly earning for themselves the historical stereotype of "bloodthirsty savages." This fallacy can be challenged when raiding is viewed as an economic necessity rather than a sadistic pastime. Hunting game for food and shelter was the most significant economic pursuit for Apaches, but raiding was also important in obtaining necessary sup-plies.[67] Glory and prestige were secondary rewards. The war party, an integral part of Apache life, had as its objective revenge.[68] Hunting, raiding, and warring were the three central features of Apache life. In order for a band to survive, both males and females participated in these activities.

There was no linguistic difference between the words for raiding and warring in the Apachean language. Each was referred to by a term meaning "they are scouting about," but there was a distinction between the two activities.[69] The sole objective of a raid was to obtain horses, cattle, weapons, ammunition, food, and, in some cases, captives. Raid-ing parties were small in number, and the participants did not actively seek out conflict.

A war party was formed when a raiding expedition or a camp was attacked and lives were lost. This necessitated a retaliatory war expedition:

> Sometimes when the Chiricahua are on the raid, the enemy kills some of their principal men. Their people whose relatives have been killed notify the leaders, warriors, and everybody — the entire encampment. Even though they are in sorrow they notify these friends to have a war dance. Following it they are going to go after the enemy, no matter where they have gone.[70]

War parties were large in number, and emotions became intense and violent. Geronimo's war parties usually numbered about seventy-five, Victorio's no more than sixty, and Nana's about twenty or thirty.[71]

Vengeance was demanded in most native American cultures, and the Apaches were no exception to the rule. James Kawaykla stated that "it was our obligation to retaliate for the wrongs inflicted upon us."[72] At times a life for a life was not considered a just revenge, and for every Apache killed many lives were taken in retaliation. Usually a relative of the deceased asked the leader of the band to organize the war party. Warriors volunteered for the expedition and relatives of the dead enlisted as many as possible of their own families, even females.[73]

Apache boys were trained as warriors at an early age. When a boy reached puberty he became an apprentice warrior. He had to accompany four raiding or warring expeditions as a novice before he could become a full-fledged warrior. There was no definite age when a boy could volunteer for his first raiding party and no one was required to volunteer, but if a boy wished to have a wife, family, material wealth, and respect from his peers, he had little choice in the matter.[74] As an apprentice warrior, a boy helped the women who accompanied the war parties. This was the only instance in which it was acceptable for a male to do domestic work. After the required four raids, the boy was usually designated a warrior. Girls did not receive the same structured warrior training as did the boys, but were taught basic hunting and warring skills in order to be prepared to fight.

Apache wives were frequent companions on raiding and warring parties. Customarily those wives who desired to accompany their husbands were allowed to do so without reservation. The wives and children of such famous Apache leaders as Chuhuahua, Juh, and Geronimo always accompanied their husbands and fathers.[75] Juh married one of Geronimo's sisters. Kawaykla remembered that she was a very shrewd and influential person who suggested much of the warriors' military strategy.[76] The primary duties of wives on raids were to remain in the temporary camp and tend to the tasks of cooking, cleaning, and nursing the wounded. Novice warriors helped them with these chores.

Women were responsible for moral and spiritual support of the male warriors. When they left for a raid, the women sent them off with applause and cheers.[77] Some women prayed for their husbands' safety, but most simply behaved with caution so as not to bring bad luck to the warriors.[78] Wives who accompanied the expeditions were discouraged from sleeping or having sexual relations with their spouses, as this was thought to hinder the husband's fighting ability, depriving him of much-needed energy for the following day's activities.[79]

If a party returned successfully, wives prepared a victory feast for the warriors. Asa Daklugie, son of Juh, related his mother's role in a victory feast after a raid into Mexico:

> Dressed in her gorgeous beaded buckskin robes, Ishton directed preparations for the feast. . . . Cooking pots were placed around the big central fire of logs, and meat was laid to roast on small beds of coals. Women baked meal cakes made of sweet acorns and piled them on wooden slabs. After my father had blown smoke in each of the four directions, he raised his arm and the women began serving the food.[80]

After the feast, the women listened to the exploits of the victorious warriors, but the women were not allowed to speak. A war dance concluded the storytelling, followed by social dances in which the women could participate.

Apache women were not strictly relegated to the domestic duties when accompanying raiding and warring parties. Many times the women had to fight in a skirmish, and they knew how to handle weapons. They were very effective warriors. Kawaykla recalled that his mother never hesitated to enter a battle with her husband and when necessary she fought beside him as bravely as any man. Kawaykla said, "my father was a brave warrior, and my mother's place was at his side."[81] In one instance her fighting skills saved her husband's life:

> Kaytennae [Gouyen's husband] leaped to the ground and dropped into an arroyo. Mother followed with me behind her. Before we could overtake Kaytennae, she had her rifle

in readiness. . . . As we passed the mouth of a side arroyo I
saw the shadow of a rifle move. . . . Kaytennae was racing
toward us, but it was Mother who got the first shot. There
was no need for another.[82]

Kawaykla also remembered an instance in which his mother expressed
her desire to encompass the role of a warrior in a more comprehensive
manner. She was resentful of Lozen, an exceptional woman warrior in
the Warm Springs band. She had distinguished herself as a great warrior and was a constant companion of the men:

> In the skirmishes and ambushes that occurred, Lozen fought
> with the warriors. Both Kaytennae and Grandfather
> praised her fighting qualities so highly that Mother was a bit
> resentful. "I could do the same if I had anyone with whom
> to leave Kawaykla," she told my stepfather.[83]

Kawaykla's mother Gouyen, and possibly many other Apache wives,
desired to take more active roles in the defense of their people, but
could not leave their children. If they so wished to fight with the men,
they were not denied the opportunity to do so.

In *Indeh: An Apache Odyssey*, May Peso Second, daughter of Mescalero Apache chief Peso, recounted the exploits of an Apache wife who
took it upon herself to avenge her husband's murder. The woman is
referred to as Gouyen. Kawaykla's mother was also called Gouyen, a
name given to those females who were virtuous, brave, and
intelligent.[84] Gouyen's husband was killed by a Comanche chief. The
Mescaleros had been hunting along the Pecos River and were surprised
by a Comanche raiding party returning from Mexico. Gouyen wished
to avenge her husband's death personally because her family had no
strong men to bear the responsibility:

> Gouyen's heart burned like a coal of living fire, a fire that
> could be quenched only by avenging her husband's death. It
> had been little more than two days since she had seen the
> tall Comanche chief stoop over his prostrate body, wave his
> bloody scalp high, and leap to the back of a black stallion
> with three white feet.[85]

Gouyen decided to go after the Comanche chief. She knew that her
family would not let her go alone, so she sneaked out of camp after
everyone was asleep. She followed the Comanches' trail for three

nights when she finally spotted the camp at night by fire and drum-
beats. Before approaching, she changed into her beaded ceremonial
dress. She slipped into the circle of dancers and began to implement her
vengeful deed:

> She circled the drummer and singers to approach the chief.
> As she stood before him with arms outstretched he recog-
> nized the universal invitation and staggered to his feet. . . .
> As they fell into the simple step of the social dance the scalp,
> swinging with the movement, steeled her to her purpose.[86]

She drew the chief away and attempted to steal his knife to use as a
weapon. The Comanche realized her intentions, and Gouyen had to
act quickly and resourcefully:

> She lifted her head and, as he bent over her, she sank her
> strong teeth into his neck and locked her arms above his el-
> bows. . . . How long she maintained her grip before the
> Comanche, staggering and fighting, fell, she did not
> know. . . . His struggles became weaker, feebler, until
> finally they ceased.[87]

When Gouyen realized that she had killed the Comanche, she went on
to exact an even bloodier revenge. Taking the man's knife, she peeled
off his scalp. She mounted a horse she had stolen and headed for her
own camp, knowing that the Comanches would be coming in search of
her. After riding for two days and nights, she lost consciousness and
was miraculously found by her tribespeople.[88]

Gouyen's story is an unusual saga of initiative, courage, and
strength. It is not representative of the behavior of most Apache wives,
but also it was not a unique occurrence. There were other stories of
women who were allowed to personally avenge the death of a family
member.

As the Chiricahua Apache bands became smaller and continued to
remain off the reservation, the women began to assume the roles of
warriors in broader and more frequent capacities. During the 1870s
and 1880s, when some Chiricahuas refused to stay on the reservations,
numerous outbreaks occurred in which entire families made up the war
parties and the women were vital participants.

Jason Betzinez, a Chiricahua Apache who fought with Geronimo,
related an incident that showed the women fulfilling a dangerous role.
The band was being attacked by Mexican troops, and the women were
digging trenches for the men:

They [the men] stood off the Mexicans while the few women
with them dug a big hole in the dry creek bed. Here they
made their stand in this rifle pit. . . . The women also dug
holes for other warriors in the bank of the little arroyo,
around the center strong point.[89]

While these women were not doing the actual fighting in this battle,
they were providing a valuable military service.

Several recorded instances tell of Apache women serving as lookouts.
When the Warm Springs band fled from the San Carlos Reservation,
women were sentries. In one episode James Kawaykla's grandmother
watched for United States troops who might have been pursuing them:

As usual, sentinels were posted in all directions. Grandmother took her place on the edge overlooking Nana's
men.[90]

Other women in the band kept lookout for enemies and made sure that
the horses were ready for traveling:

Siki, Mother, and Blanco's wife checked the horses, tied
their equipment to the saddles, and hobbled their mounts.
Mother was the first to spy the riders, tiny specks moving
toward the canyon.[91]

These women were performing double duty, not only executing tasks
often assigned to male warriors, but also keeping a close watch on the
children and elderly members of the band, nursing the wounded, and
tending to the domestic chores of tanning, sewing, and cooking.

After Victorio was killed, Nana regrouped the survivors and made
his way to the border. The band desperately needed horses, and fortunately they came across two vaqueros with a herd of horses. Kawaykla's
mother and four other women rode with the warriors on the successful
raid.[92] Two other women who accompanied Nana's warriors were
highly skilled nurses and efficient fighters. They were not required to
cook and do other chores usually done by the wives who accompanied
their husbands.[93]

Some Chiricahua Apache women were asked to kill and torture captives. One of Morris Opler's Apache informants related such instances;

They say they used to tie Mexicans with their hands behind
their backs. Then they turned the women loose with axes

> and knives to kill the Mexican prisoner. The man could hardly run, and the women would chase him around until they killed him. . . . When a brave warrior is killed, the men go out for about three Mexicans. They bring them back for the women to kill in revenge. The women ride at them on horseback, armed with spears.[94]

This practice, probably not a frequent occurrence, is unusual in that women were the primary perpetrators of the violence.

An Apache woman who held a less violent but very dangerous and important position was Dahteste or Tah-das-te. The wife of Chiricahua Apache warrior Anandia, she accompanied him on raiding and warring parties. She was admired and fought beside the men in ambushes and attacks. She traveled with Geronimo's band as messenger. Lozen usually accompanied her, and the women acted as go-betweens for Geronimo and numerous United States military officers. When Geronimo's band was being pursued by Lieutenant Gatewood and his troops, the two women were sent to negotiate. According to members of the band, Lozen and Dahteste arranged a conference with Captain Emmett Crawford concerning the band's famous 1886 surrender.[95] Military accounts state that "two women or squaws" came into camp to deliver messages from Geronimo.[96] Other military reports show that the women negotiated with Lieutenant Britton Davis, Lieutenant Charles B. Gatewood, and General Nelson E. Miles.[97] The advantages in sending Lozen and Dahteste as messengers were that they posed a less threatening presence to the American military leaders than would males, and many Apache men at this time were being employed by the military to serve as scouts and lead the American troops to Apache hideouts. American male officers were unlikely to enlist two women as scouts, even though they would have been mentally and physically capable of the task. The grave responsibilities associated with delivering vital messages demonstrates the immense trust and respect that Geronimo held for Dahteste and Lozen.

Dahteste was with Geronimo when the band surrendered.[98] Her husband at the time, Anandia, left her while they were being held in Alabama and returned to a previous wife.[99] She then married Coonie or Kuni, who was an Apache scout at Fort Apache. His wife had died and left him with three children. Dahteste was his last wife, and in addition to Coonie's children, reared three of his nephews. She lived on the Mescalero Reservation until her death.[100] She is remembered as a brave and valuable woman warrior.

The **Chiricahua Tah-des-te**, messenger and warrior in Geronimo's band. She and Lozen negotiated with several American military leaders. She surrendered with Geronimo in 1886. (With permission of Eve Ball, from her *In the Days of Victorio: Recollections of a Warm Spring Apache*, 1970.)

Ishton, Gouyen, Dahteste and many other Chiricahua Apache wives justly earned the title of warrior by their courage, daring, and skill in areas that were traditionally considered as male domains. They were valuable members of hunting, raiding, and warring parties, whether in their domestic or military capacities. It is obvious that all Chiricahua Apache women did not choose to fight beside their husbands, but they were definitely not reluctant to do whatever was necessary when an adversary attacked. Women and men valiantly fought together in the Apache struggle for survival. "If a woman dearly loved her husband," said Ace Daklugie, "she fought beside him."[101] Some women were forced into the roles of warriors, while for others it was a matter of choice.

CHAPTER FOUR

LOZEN: WARRIOR

LOZEN IS AS MY RIGHT HAND. STRONG AS A MAN, BRAVER THAN
MOST, AND CUNNING IN STRATEGY, LOZEN IS A SHIELD TO HER
PEOPLE.

Victorio[102]

· Lozen was an extraordinary woman in the history of the Apaches because she is the only known unmarried woman to be allowed to accompany warring and raiding parties in an active capacity on a permanent
basis. Apache wives were able to go with their husbands on raids and
war parties but only because they were married to warriors, or when
an expedition's purpose was to avenge the loss of one of their family
members. These women did not fully encompass the role of a warrior
as did Lozen. Kawaykla remembered Victorio saying, "I depend upon
Lozen as I do Nana."[103] The Apaches contend that they had not spoken
of Lozen to non-Indians until recent times because they feared she
would be ridiculed or misunderstood for her lifestyle.[104] A courageous
and magnificent warrior, she was never ridiculed or ostracized by her
contemporaries for riding with the men. They deeply respected her and
reverently called her "The Woman Warrior." ·

·Lozen was said to be the younger sister of Warm Springs chief Victorio, but she may have been his cousin, as there was no separate term

for sibling or silah in the Apachean language. Cousins were often referred to as brothers and sisters. Morris Opler explained the ambiguity
of the terms:

> Sikis literally signifies "sibling or cousin of the same sex as
> myself,: and silah carries the force of "sibling or cousin of
> the opposite sex from myself." Thus, when a woman says
> sikis, she is speaking of a sister or female cousin; when a man
> uses the same term, he has in mind a brother or a male
> cousin. Conversely, when a man says silah, he is referring to
> a sister or a female cousin.[105]

The silah relationship was a very delicate social matter. As soon as
Apache children were old enough to understand social amenities they
learned that a "certain decorum" had to be observed in the presence of
a silah.[106] Opler stated that "Brothers and sisters feel so uncomfortable
in each other's company that they do not court situations which will
throw them together."[107] One Apache informant told Opler that "the
avoidance of cousins of the opposite sex starts when they are old enough
to understand such things, when they have grown to maturity, and
lasts all their lives."[108]

The traditional silah avoidance practice seems to pose a problem in
the open acceptance of Lozen's familial relationship to Victorio and
her concurrent role as his companion on raiding and warring expeditions. However, when the extreme pressures confronting the Warm
Springs band in that period (1869-81) are considered, the possibility of
the close relationship which defied the traditional silah decorum can be
explained. The band was faced with two equally distressing alter-
natives in the 1870s: captivity or flight. Victorio and his people chose to
remain free and retain their nomadic lifestyle. They spent their days
with the constant threat of attack and annihilation from Mexican and
American civilians and troops. Many traditions, including the silah
avoidance practice, were altered or perhaps even totally abandoned
while the band was struggling for survival. Everyone's welfare depend-
ed entirely upon intercommunication and close contact. Strict
adherence to the traditional silah avoidance practice was not only in-
feasible, but life-threatening.

Lozen chose to digress from the traditional social norm for females
when she decided to pursue the life of a full-time warrior in lieu of the
roles of wife and mother. An Apache story explains her choice. Lozen
was about sixteen years old when the band gave refuge to a stranger.

He said he was a chief of the Seneca tribe from New York, seeking a home in the south for his people.[109] Lozen fell in love with this man, whom the Apaches call Gray Wolf or Gray Ghost. He continued on his journey and left his young admirer broken hearted. After this she refused all suitors and her wish to remain single was respected.

This story is not historically verifiable; conceivably the tale has been used by the Apaches as a means of protecting Lozen from those who would label her as a lesbian or transvestite. It could also be a romanticized love story. There is, however, the strong possibility that a member of the Seneca tribe was in New Mexico. From the memories of James Kawaykla, it is possible to place Lozen's birthdate in the late 1840s.[110] According to the Gray Wolf story, Lozen fell in love before going through her puberty ceremony or around her sixteenth birthday. This would roughly place Gray Wolf's presence in New Mexico in the late 1850s or 1860s. During this time the Senecas were in a state of upheaval in their New York homeland. The federal government was trying to force them onto reservations in Kansas or lands further south.[111] Some were moved to Kansas, but others went in search of new land. Gray Wolf could have been in New Mexico seeking a southwestern haven for his people.

Since the authenticity of the Gray Wolf story is unsubstantiated, it has been suggested that the Apaches tell the story to refute questions of Lozen's sexual preferences and/or promiscuity. It is unlikely that Lozen was a transvestite, morphadite, lesbian, or prostitute. Morris Opler quoted Apache informants as saying there were a number of women who excelled in activities commonly considered the interests of men, but who were not considered transvestites.[112] Another added, "All girls were urged to be strong and fast. It was simply accepted that these particular individuals have carried the requirements further than is strictly necessary."[113] Homosexuality was forbidden and ridiculed in Apache society.[114] Sexual promiscuity was frowned upon by Apaches, and prostitutes were practically unheard of among their bands. Since Lozen was held in such high esteem by her peers, the likelihood of her exercising such roles is very slim, if not impossible.

Lozen was an excellent equestrian, known for her horsemanship skills among her own people and with the American military personnel as well. She was skillful at stampeding and stealing horses and was also an expert roper. These abilities made her an invaluable member of raiding parties. Her prowess as a horse thief is apparent in this excerpt from *In the Days of Victorio:*

Apache prisoners of war, taken in 1886 near the Nueces River in Texas. The prisoners were being transported to Florida by the Southern Pacific line. Lozen is third from the right in the top row; Geronimo is third from right in the bottom row. (With permission of Eve Ball, from her *In the Days of Victorio,* 1970.)

When the guard left the horses and started toward the fire
she must make her attempt to secure one. Already she had
selected a powerful steed, one of the most restless. When the
guard had passed the fire she would tie her leather rope
around its lower jaw, cut the hobbles and ride. She crept
softly to the animal, and quickly tied the rope. . . . She
leaped to its back and turned it toward the river. Bullets
whizzed past her head as the horse slid down the bank and
plunged into the water.[115]

John C. Cremony, a southwestern cavalry officer, kept extensive records of his encounters with the Apaches. He recorded that an Apache
woman was "renowned as one of the most dextrous horse thieves and
horse breakers in the tribe, and seldom permitted an expedition to go
on a raid without her presence."[116] He could not recall her Apache
name, although he remembered the translation as being "Dextrous
Horse Thief" and that she "was one who received particular honor
from the other sex."[117] This description certainly fit Lozen.

Bravery and skill were two of Lozen's most admired qualities. She
was quick to see where her services were needed and equally quick to
respond. Kawaykla stated that "She lives solely to aid him [Victorio]
and her people."[118] When the band fled the San Carlos Reservation in
1880, she led the women and children to safety. After they had safely
reached the other side of a river that had been blocking their escape
path, she left to join the men. She always carried a rifle, cartridge belt,
and knife, as did many other women.[119] She was a formidable oppo-
nent for any foe and according to Kawaykla she once "singlehandedly
killed a longhorn steer with only a knife."[120]

Lozen was not with the main Warm Springs group in Mexico when
Victorio was killed. She had temporarily left the band to help a young
Mescalero Apache woman return to the reservation in New Mexico. After Lozen had safely delivered her ward, she trailed her people to Mexico where she learned of the Tres Castillos massacre and the death of her
brother.[121] She remained with the surviving members of Victorio's
band, and rode with them and Nana on the many raids to avenge the
deaths of their tribespeople.

After raiding with Nana for a time, Lozen joined a band that oper-
ated out of the Sierra Madre mountain range. It consisted of a number
of Chiricahua Apaches from different bands. Their leader was Geronimo, the famous Apache medicine man. The band eluded Mexican and
American troops and constantly raided throughout northern Mexico,

Arizona, and New Mexico. Lozen was accepted as a valuable warrior. She was given the name "The Woman Warrior" while with Geronimo's band.[122] ·

In a desperate battle with Mexican troops, Lozen played a memorable role. She was traveling with a party of Geronimo's warriors, led by Fun, when they were attacked. During the battle she crawled into the line of fire to rescue a badly-needed pouch of ammunition that had been dropped. She successfully claimed the bullets and retreated to safety.[123] Jason Betzinez, a member of Geronimo's band, although he did not identify Lozen by name, described an Apache woman who during a battle with Mexican troops, rescued a sack of 500 cartridges which had been dropped by a runner.[124]

When Geronimo surrendered, Lozen was among his band. In April 1887 Lozen, with the other Apache prisoners of war, was moved to Mount Vernon Barracks, Alabama. Although official records cannot be located (the census from Mount Vernon Barracks only lists the prisoners by number and Lozen was not ever officially recognized as one of the prisoners), Eugene Chihuahua, a fellow Apache prisoner, remembered the details of Lozen's death there:

> At that time, because of the sputum we thought that that patient had worms in the lungs and that they caused the illness. . . . I think that the Army doctor, too, tried to cure Chapo. But as did many others, he died. Lozen, sister of chief Victorio, died of the same sickness. She also died at Mt. Vernon.[125]

Lozen's death came as a poignant end to a magnificent life. She died of tuberculosis in the confinement of a white man's prison far from her beloved homeland, denied the honorable death of a warrior in battle. In keeping with Apache custom, she was secretly buried. The Apaches' decision to remain silent about her for so long kept her contributions hidden for almost a century. Now it is possible to study this remarkable woman's life and reveal her extraordinary exploits. Lozen successfully conquered a predominantly male domain, and survived as a legend.

CHAPTER FIVE

lozen
aNd
OTHER ApACHE WOMEN:
SHAMANS

With outstretched hands Lozen would slowly turn as she sang
a prayer:

> UPON THIS EARTH
> ON WHICH WE LIVE
> USSEN HAS POWER.
> THIS POWER IS MINE
> FOR LOCATING THE ENEMY.
> I SEARCH FOR THAT ENEMY
> WHICH ONLY USSEN THE GREAT
> CAN SHOW TO ME.

> James Kawaykla[126]

• Perhaps the most outstanding of Lozen's abilities was her Power. Supernatural power was a dominating theme in Apache culture, and according to Morris Opler, power was "in the largest sense, the animating

principle of the universe, the life force" of Apache society.[127] Women were not excluded from possessing power, and there were many Apache medicine women or shamans.

Apaches who possessed power were referred to as shamans or medicine men or medicine women. Shamans were numerous among the Apaches and supernatural power was attainable by everyone. An Apache informant told Opler that "supernatural power is something that every Chiricahua can share. Most of the people have some sort of ceremony, little or big."[128] An Apache child was first taught of the principal supernatural beings and the mystery surrounding power at a very early age. According to one of Opler's informants, power was essential in understanding every aspect of life:

> If we aren't shamans or have no supernatural power, we have no basis to stand on in saying how far from us the clouds are or how far away the sun is. A person like myself will tell you that rain comes from the clouds, because I have no vision about it, but others will say their power causes it.[129]

Everything in nature and everyday life was a result of supernatural power. Not fully understood by the Apaches, it was considered an omnipotent force.

⋅ Almost every imaginable occasion involved supernatural power and the services of a shaman. A female shaman was usually present at the delivery of an infant. She prayed, sang, and performed the essential ceremonies that insured the good health of the newborn baby and mother. Her presence was not absolutely necessary, but Apaches relied so heavily upon religious ritual that a shaman's services were customarily sought. Many shamans were well paid for their services and achieved a high degree of prestige and wealth.

Power was not an exclusive privilege, but the most respected shamans were those whose cures were consistently successful and whose prophecies were found to be reliable. Power was to be used for the benefit of the entire tribe, not for selfish purposes. Those who used power for evil were considered witches and/or sorcerers.[130] They were deeply feared and were usually banned from the rest of the group. Some recorded instances tell of the banishment of witches and sorcerers.[131]

Some Apaches actively sought power, while others were surprised when it came to them. Many went to older shamans and studied their procedures in an effort to acquire power. Serious obligations accompanied the acceptance of power and it was not a responsibility to be taken lightly. Power was believed to possess a force of its own, a force that could be capable of violence or vengeance.[132] A person could refuse to accept power, but this was very unusual. Power usually made its initial presence known with a spoken word or a sign. Later it might take on a human or animal form and directly communicate with the recipient.[133] It could appear at any time in a person's life, but an Apache rarely received it before puberty. Most received their power while adolescents.[134]

Warm Springs Apaches who wished to receive power traveled to the Sacred Mountain, Salinas Peak, the highest peak in the San Andreas mountain range.[135] Those traveling there approached in fear and awe for it was there that "the Mountain Spirits dwelt, they who were the link between Ussen and the Earth People."[136] The Mountain Spirits were described in legends as the "sources of supernatural power and as protectors of the tribal territory."[137]

A person going to the Sacred Mountain usually consulted with an older shaman about the journey.[138] Upon reaching the peak, the person fasted for four days and nights while the Mountain Spirits tested his or her worthiness. Those who made the trip did so alone and were forbidden to speak of it. They had to prove their courage by enduring hunger, fear, and other feats of stamina.[139] The person seeking power had to convince the Mountain Spirits that he or she could endure long fasts, interpret omens, and exercise an adequate amount of spiritual intensity.[140] After proving this worthiness, the individual would then receive a healing power, the ability to perform prophetical ceremonies, or other extraordinary powers.[141] In some instances a person did not receive power after visiting the Sacred Mountain, but most who endured the vigil were given power on the last night of the ordeal.[142]

The Apaches put great faith in the abilities of those who received and exercised power. Power was not understood or respected by most non-Indians who came into contact with them. Lieutenant James S. Pettit reported with surprise in his 1886 journal, that the Apache scouts serving in his cavalry unit relied on their own medicine men for healing, rather than consulting the military physicians:

> The Apache scouts seem to prefer their own medicine men when seriously ill, and believe the weird singing and praying around the couch is more effective than the medicine dealt out by our camp sawbones.[143]

The Apaches respected power, not only for its medicinal and healing abilities, but also for its leadership value. Asa Daklugie explained the significance of power to Apache leaders:

> Unless they believe their leader has Power he's out of luck. Of all the chiefs I knew, Naiche, when young, was the only one who had no Power.[144]

The Apaches believed that Geronimo could predict the future and was protected from injuries. He was not a true chief, but his power was so respected, he led as a chief would. Juh was said to be able to foretell the future, as well as successfully lead his people. Chief Chihuahua was believed to have had power over horses and Nana was reputed to possess power over ammunition trains and rattlesnakes.[145] Supernatural power was so important in Apache life, that it was a prerequisite to respect and leadership.

Most native American women, including Apaches, could possess power and did so when the opportunity presented itself. The only ceremonial privileges associated with power that were denied Apache women were the use of sweat lodges and the impersonation of the Mountain Spirits during ceremonial dances.[146] Most women possessed healing powers, but some had more spectacular abilities.

Captain John G. Bourke, aide to General George C. Crook during the Apache campaigns of 1870-75 and 1884-86, recalled two Apache medicine women. He identified one as "Captain Jack."[147] He did not elaborate on her powers, but did specifically describe her as an "Apache medicine-woman."[148] He also wrote of Tze-go-juni or Pretty Mouth, a Chiricahua Apache believed to have been a shaman because she narrowly escaped death on two separate occasions. Once she survived an attacking mountain lion, and then she survived being struck by lightning. She was said to have the power of escaping injury.[149] Bourke noted that the Apaches considered both women to be powerful shamans whose usual duties were dealing with obstetrical matters.[150]

James Kawaykla remembered the special powers of his mother, grandmother, and female cousin. His mother was believed to have had the power of avoiding injuries. He stated that "in all the skirmishes in which she fought . . . she never got a scratch."[151] Siki, Kawaykla's cousin, possessed a similar power, and was believed to be able to escape from her enemies without harm.[152] Kawaykla's grandmother, a sister of Nana, was said to have had the power of healing wounds.[153]

Lozen had powers that enabled her to heal wounds, and more significantly, to locate the enemy. Kawaykla noted that his people "knew her wisdom and her ability as a warrior, but most of all they respected her Power."[154] As a young woman, she frequently visited older shamans and learned from them. She traveled to the Sacred Mountain and underwent the vigil. On the fourth night she was awarded her exceptional powers.[155]

Morris Opler's Apache interviewees were very familiar with the power of locating the enemy. Opler stated that the ceremonial procedure of this type was generally referred to as "it moves the arms about."[156] This was the ceremony that James Kawaykla saw Lozen perform on several occasions. He remembered that Lozen would search out the direction and distance of the enemy as she stood with her face turned toward the sky and her arms outstretched. She would then sing the prayer that is printed at the opening of this chapter or she sometimes used this prayer:

> In this world Ussen has Power;
> This Power He has granted me
> For the good of my people.
> This I see as one from a height
> Sees in every direction;
> This I feel as though I
> Held in my palms something that tingles.
> This Power is mine to use,
> But only for the good of my people.[157]

As she sang, she would slowly move in a circle until a tingling sensation in her palms signaled the enemy's location. Kawaykla also recalled that her palms would almost become purple when she located the pursuers.[158] Her powers were deeply respected. Many of the Warm Springs band fervently believed that Victorio never would have been killed at Tres Castillos had Lozen been there to warn him of the enemy.[159]

Lozen or another shaman always accompanied the expeditions of Victorio, Nana, and Geronimo. Some were believed to have the power to halt the enemy; others could provide protection from attack and still others were assumed to be able to control the weather or the length of the day and the night. One or more shamans were consulted by the leader of a party in most major decisions. The shaman usually brought up the rear of a party so that he or she could perform the ceremonies.[160] Many a battle was waged on the advice and consent of a shaman.

Power was instrumental in all phases of Apache life. Shamans were extremely influential individuals. Many documented stories describe female shamans in native American societies. Lozen's role as an exceptionally important Apache shaman, gained for her an enormous amount of freedom and respect. Supernatural power was a significant means by which native American women gained status, prestige, and leadership among their people.

CHAPTER SIX

WOMEN WARRIORS: forgotten gladiators

IN FEW OTHER NON-WESTERN SOCIETIES WERE SOME WOMEN
ABLE TO PARTICIPATE SO READILY IN THOSE MALE ACTIVITIES
THAT LED TO HIGH PRESTIGE.

Katherine Weist[161]

A careful review of the historical and anthropological literature shows that not only Apache women, but many native American women were active participants in martial activities. Their roles encompassed a diverse range of experiences. Some wives were camp followers who remained in the temporary shelter while their husbands did the actual raiding and fighting. Other women performed the vital and dangerous duties of digging trenches, delivering important messages, and serving as sentries. Female shamans were highly respected for their supernatural powers and often were valuable participants in warring and raiding expeditions. Some females who were especially independent and strong, became warriors in the fullest sense of the word and were legends among their people.

Many Sioux women, openly and secretly, accompanied men on war parties. Most of these women participated in only one skirmish, then returned to their domestic duties. Revenge was the common motive for a Sioux woman to join a war party. She would ride with the men to avenge the death of husband, brother, or other close relative.[162] Accounts of individual exploits of most of these women have not survived, but this should not detract from the contributions of those who did ride as warriors.

The Kutenai or Kootenay people tell of a woman who gave up the traditional female lifestyle of wife and mother to hunt and fight with the men. Unlike the other women warriors described in this study, she completely absorbed her male identity, and ultimately took another woman for a wife. Water-sitting Grizzly or Bowdash is mentioned in several books and journals of early traders and travelers.[163] A description of her can be found in Beverly Hungry Wolf's *The Ways of My Grandmothers* in quotations from Claude Schaeffer's unpublished field notes:

> She was to become not only the most publicized personage of early Kutenai history, but, next to Sacajawea [a Shoshone woman who guided the white explorers Lewis and Clark through her tribal country of long ago], perhaps the best-known Plateau Indian woman of the period. . . . Water-sitting Grizzly, as she became known to her people, married Thompson's servant, Boisverd, in 1808. He took her to a fur post, probably Kootenae House, to live. There her conduct became so loose, contrary to Kutenai standards, that Thompson was compelled to send her home. Madame Boisverd explained to her people that the white man had changed her sex, by virtue of which she had acquired a spiritual power. Thereafter she assumed a masculine name, donned men's clothing and weapons, adopted manly pursuits, and took a woman as wife.[164]

An excerpt from the 1837 journal of W.H. Gray, a Protestant missionary, reported that a "Kutenai transvestite" whom he called Bowdash was a member of a party of Flathead Indians who were surrounded by attacking Blackfeet. Bowdash served as a mediator to the Blackfeet while her people made their escape. When the Blackfeet discovered her scheme she was killed.[165]

The Blackfeet have a renowned woman warrior of their own. Running Eagle is the most extolled woman in the history of the Blackfoot Nation. She was a great warrior and many Blackfeet men referred to her as a chief. Unmarried, she was regarded as a holy woman who put up Sun Dances, a task previously reserved for males.[166] Running Eagle's unusual life is recounted in *The Ways of My Grandmothers:*

The popular story is that Running Eagle began life as an ordinary Blackfoot girl named Brown Weasel Woman. She had two brothers and two sisters, and her father was a well-known warrior. When she became of the age that boys begin to practice hunting, she asked her father to make a set of bow and arrows with which she could practice. . . . It was during one of the buffalo hunts with her father that this unusual girl is said to have first shown her warrior's courage. . . . Brown Weasel Woman's father had his horse shot out from under him. One of the bravest deeds performed by warriors in the old days was to brave the enemy fire while riding back to rescue a companion who was left on foot. This is what the daughter did for her father.[167]

Running Eagle's father was eventually killed during another battle and soon afterward her mother died. The young woman then decided to pursue the life of a warrior.

Her first encounter came soon after her parents' deaths. She accompanied a war party to avenge the theft of some horses. The men did not want her to go, but a cousin of the girl accepted responsibility for her. The raid on a Crow camp was successful and Brown Weasel Woman was credited with the capture of eleven horses.[168] After the raid, she was stationed as a sentry when a group camped overnight. She spotted two enemy riders and dealt with them in such a way that she won the respect of even the most dubious male:

Then, as the enemies closed in on her, expecting no trouble from a woman, she shot the one who carried a rifle and forced the other one to turn and try an escape. Instead of reloading her own rifle, she ran and grabbed the one from the fallen enemy, and shot after the one getting away. She missed him, but others of the party went after him and shortly brought him down as well.[169]

Running Eagle, like Lozen, possessed supernatural power that increased her value as a warrior. After Running Eagle had ridden on her first war expedition, she sought a vision and was rewarded with the power that "men consider necessary for leading a successful warrior's life."[170] She also was allowed to speak at the Medicine Lodge ceremony, another privilege that had before been exclusively limited to males, and occasionally the wife of a warrior. She was given the name Running Eagle, a name reserved for famous Blackfoot warriors, at a medicine lodge ceremony. The Braves Society of Young Warriors then invited and accepted her as a member.[171]

Chief Earth Woman, an Ojibwa warrior, is a significant figure in Ojibwa history. Her story has many parallels to those of Lozen and Running Eagle. It was not unusual for women to accompany Ojibwa war parties. Some of the young women went on campaigns with their fathers and served as rewards for the male warriors who performed well in battle.[172] Chief Earth Woman did not accompany war parties in this capacity:

> Chief Earth Woman's first military enterprise was inspired by her love for a young warrior, who unfortunately was already married. . . . But Chief Earth Woman still flirted with the handsome young brave, and when he and the other men made plans to attack the Sioux, she decided she wanted to go along. . . . The spunky maiden was able to convince the leader of the war party to allow her to continue by confiding to him that she had had a dream that gave her special supernatural powers. Indeed she was able to predict the movements of the Sioux. . . . When the Ojibwas surprised the Sioux, Chief Earth Woman's lover was the first to kill one of the enemy, and she ran up to the victim as soon as he fell and took his scalp off. When the war party returned to their camp . . . she was given the traditional honors just like her male companions.[173]

Whether Chief Earth Woman continued her warring lifestyle is not known. She was indeed a woman warrior who earned her title.

Cheyenne women did not usually accompany war parties, but several were recognized as warriors. Accounts tell of females who risked their lives in order to rescue their male relatives during battle.[174] One told of Buffalo Calf Road Woman or Muts-i-mi-u-na who saved her brother in a battle with the Sioux. She gained much recognition for her deed, and the Cheyenne referred to this battle by the name "Where the girl saved the brother."[175]

The most famous Cheyenne woman warrior is Ehyophsta or Yellow-Haired Woman, most remembered for her role in an 1868 battle with the Shoshoni. During the battle she killed one Shoshoni and counted coup on another. After the fighting, one young Shoshoni warrior who had survived the battle was discovered. Ehyophsta stepped forward, lifted up his arm, and thrust her knife into his armpit, then scalped him.[176] Her exploits gained her entrance into a small society of Cheyenne women who had fought in war.[177]

The Cherokee were so respectful of their women warriors they created a special office for them called Ghi-ga-u, a word meaning Beloved Woman, Pretty Woman, or War Woman.[178] The war women attended every council and offered advice on strategy and other military matters. They became eligible for the office by their military deeds. Many were also the mothers of warriors. One of their main duties was to determine the fate of condemned captives.[179] The office of Ghi-ga-u served as a powerful impetus for many Cherokee females to become warriors.

Clearly women warriors were active participants in many native American societies. The oral traditions of these remarkable women have survived through the years, though many others have unfortunately been lost in the silence of history. There are stories of women warriors among the Apache, Sioux, Kutenai, Blackfoot, Ojibwa, Cheyenne, Cherokee, Crow, Gros Ventres, Mandan, Pawnee and possibly numerous other tribes. These sagas reveal striking similarities. They recount the exploits of wives, sisters, or cousins who ignored personal danger and unselfishly rescued male relatives during battles. The most prestigious women warriors were usually young, unmarried, and possessed supernatural powers that in some way helped to insure the success of war parties. Most of the women warriors lived in societies that relied on hunting and raiding as their mainstays. Largely nomadic peoples, they followed the available game supply. This environment more readily lent itself to flexible sex roles and a more open acceptance of those females who chose to enter the traditional male domains.

Status has been defined as "the degree to which a person possesses characteristics valued in a particular society.[180] Female status has been shown to increase when "conditions favor significant participation by females in either [political or economic] sphere for an extended period of time."[181] A power base is said to develop when females significantly participate in "subsistence or warfare activities."[182] If status and power are indeed determined by these variables, then the women warriors examined in this study enjoyed a very high status and held a firm power base among their people, two observations that are conclusively valid. It is safe to say that Apache women, as a whole, exercised considerable power and independence as well.

Women warriors gained respect and status because their respective societies gave them the opportunities to strive for pursuits traditionally considered to be reserved for males. Apache women and other native American women were not denied access to these roles, and many chose to embrace them. This phenomenon cannot be observed in such a comprehensive manner in most other eighteenth- and nineteenth-century non-Indian North American cultures, especially Anglo-American societies. Native American women warriors were a significant group who exercised tremendous courage, individuality, and power. The accomplishments of such women as Ishton, Gouyen, Dahteste, Running Eagle, Chief Earth Woman, and Lozen demand a revision of the drab stereotype that belittles the image of native American women.

NOTES

1 Eve Ball, *In the Days of Victorio: Recollections of a Warm Springs Apache* (Tucson: University of Arizona Press, 1970), 62.

2 James L. Haley, *Apaches: A History and Culture Portrait* (Garden City, N.Y.: Doubleday and Co., 1981), 3.

3 Haley, *Apaches*, 10.

4 James H. Gunnerson, "Southern Athapaskan Archaeology," in *The Handbook of North American Indians*, gen. ed. W.C. Sturtevant (Washington, D.C.: Smithsonian Institution, 1979), 163; Haley, *Apaches*, 10.

5 Gunnerson, "Southern Athapaskan," 163; Haley, *Apaches*, 10.

6 Albert H. Schroeder, *Apache Indians: A Study of Apache Indians*, parts I, II and III (New York: Garland Press, Inc., 1974), 80.

7 Ibid.

8 John Upton Terrell, *Apache Chronicle* (New York: World Publishing Co., 1972), 35.

9 Gunnerson, "Southern Athapaskan," 162.

10 Michael E. Melody, *The Apaches: A Critical Bibliography* (Bloomington: Indiana University Press, 1977), 3.

11 Haley, *Apaches*, 9; Schroeder, *Apache Indians*, 32.

12 Greenville Goodwin, *The Social Organization of the Western Apache* (Chicago: University of Chicago Press, 1942), 1.

13 Gunnerson, "Southern Athapaskan," 162.

14 Ball, *In the Days*, xiv.

15 Schroeder, *Apache Indians*, 43.

16 Donald E. Worcester, *The Apaches: Eagles of the Southwest* (Norman: University of Oklahoma Press, 1979), 10.

17 Ibid., 21.

18 Ibid., 37-38.

19 Dan L. Thrapp, *Victorio and the Mimbres Apaches* (Norman: University of Oklahoma Press, 1967), 19.

20 Ibid.

21 Ibid.

22 Ibid., 21.

23 Ibid., 24.

24 Ibid., 25.

25 Charles J. Kappler, *Indian Affairs, Laws and Treaties*, vol. II (Washington, D.C.: General Printing Office, 1904), 598.

26 Ibid., 599.

27 Thrapp, *Victorio*, 182.

28 Ibid., 193.

29 Ibid., 203.

30 Thomas E. Mails, *The People Called Apache* (Englewood Cliffs, N.J.: Prentice Hall, 1974), 214.

31 Haley, *Apaches*, 332.

32 Ibid., 334.

33 Ibid., 332.

34 Ibid.

35 U.S. Congress, *Report of the Secretary of War*, 50th Cong., 1st sess., 1887, 71.

36 U.S. Congress, *Senate Executive Document 117*, 49th Cong., 2nd sess., 1886, 4.

37 Ibid., 22-30.

38 Geronimo, *Geronimo's Story of his Life*, ed. S. M. Barrett (New York: Duffield and Co., 1915), 145; Angie Debo, *Geronimo: The Man, His Time, His Place* (Norman: University of Oklahoma Press, 1976), 301, 309.

39 U.S. Congress, *Report of the Secretary of War*, 50th Cong., 1st sess., 1889, 158.

40 Ibid.

41 Ibid.

42 Ball, *In the Days*, 21.

43 Carolyn Niethammer, *Daughters of the Earth: The Lives and Legends of American Indian Women* (New York: Macmillan Publishing Co., Inc., 1977), xii.

44 Goodwin, *Social Organization*, 537, 540; Morris E. Opler, *An Apache Life-Way* (Chicago: University of Chicago Press, 1941), 63, 162-63.

45 Opler, *Life-Way*, 63.

46 Ibid., 163.

47 Ibid., 161-66.

48 Niethammer, *Daughters*, 107.

49 Mails, *The People*, 214.

50 Ball, *In the Days*, 66.

51 Opler, *Life-Way*, 75.

52 Ibid.

53 Ibid.

54 Ball, *In the Days*, 5-6.

55 Ibid., 113.

56 Opler, *Life-Way*, 48.

57 Ibid., 75-76.

58 Ibid., 201.

59 Ibid., 194.

60 Eve Ball and Lynda Sánchez, "Legendary Apache Women," *Frontier Times* (October-November 1980), 8.

61 Janice DeLaney, Mary Jane Lupton, and Emily Toth, *The Curse: A Cultural History of Menstruation* (New York: C. P. Dutton & Co., inc., 1976), 5.

62 Ibid.

63 Opler, *Life-Way*, 80.

64 Ibid., 81.

65 Ibid., 82.

66 Ball, *In the Days*, 9.

67 Opler, *Life-Way*, 334.

68 Ibid.

69 Ibid., 333.

70 Ibid., 335.

71 James Betzinez with Wilbur Sturtevant Nye, *I Fought with Geronimo* (Harrisburg, Pa.: The Stackpole Co., 1959), 6.

72 Ball, *In the Days*, 119.

73 Mails, *The People*, 252.

74 Ibid., 260-61.

75 Ball, *Indeh*, 47, 103.
76 Ball, *In the Days*, 127.
77 Opler, *Life-Way*, 342.
78 Ibid., 342-43.
79 Ball, *Indeh*, 104.
80 Ibid., 8.
81 Ball, *In the Days*, 8.
82 Ibid., 110.
83 Ibid., 120.
84 Ball, *Indeh*, 204.
85 Ibid.
86 Ibid., 208.
87 Ibid., 209.
88 Ibid., 209-10.
89 Betzinez, *Geronimo*, 73.
90 Ball, *In the Days*, 12.
91 Ibid., 13.
92 Ibid., 103.
93 Ibid., 108.
94 Opler, *Life-Way*, 351.
95 Ball, *In the Days*, 182.
96 Brigadier General James Parker, "The Geronimo Campaign," in *The Papers of the Order of Indian Wars* (Fort Collins, Colo.: The Old Army Press, 1975), 100. Lieutenant Charles B. Gatewood, "The Surrender of Geronimo," in *The Papers of the Order of Indian Wars*, 107.
97 Nelson A. Miles, *Personal Recollections and Observations of General Nelson A. Miles* (New York and Chicago: 1896; reprint ed., New York: DaCapo Press, 1969), 456, 464, 511.
98 Gillett Griswold, comp., "The Fort Sill Apaches: Their Vital Statistics, Tribal Origins, Antecedents" (U.S. Army Field Artillery and Fort Sill Museum, Fort Sill, Okla., 1958-62), 130; Woodward B. Skinner, letter to author, 7 February 1983.
99 Griswold, "Fort Sill Apaches," 130.
100 Ball and Sánchez, "Women," 11.
101 Ibid., 10.
102 Ball, *In the Days*, 15.
103 Ibid.
104 Ball, *Indeh*, 104n.
105 Opler, *Life-Way*, 58.
106 Ibid., 59.
107 Ibid., 60.
108 Ibid., 61.
109 Ball and Sánchez, "Women," 11; Ball, *In the Days*, 14.
110 Ball, *In the Days*, 115.
111 Kappler, *Affairs*, 960.
112 Opler, *Life-Way*, 416.
113 Ibid.
114 Ibid., 415.
115 Ball, *In the Days*, 117.

116 John C. Cremony, *Life Among the Apaches* (1868; reprint, Glorieta, N. Mex.: Rio Grande Press, Inc., 1969), 243.

117 Ibid.

118 Ball, *In the Days*, 14.

119 Ibid., 116.

120 Ibid.

121 Ibid., 119-20.

122 Ball and Sánchez, "Women," 10.

123 Ball, *Indeh*, 155.

124 Betzinez, *Geronimo*, 73-74.

125 Ball, *Indeh*, 154.

126 Ball, *In the Days*, 15.

127 Opler, *Life-Way*, 205.

128 Ibid., 200.

129 Ibid., 36.

130 Ibid., 252-53.

131 Ball, *In the Days*, 16; Opler, *Life-Way*, 252-53.

132 Opler, *Life-Way*, 203, 255.

133 Ibid., 204.

134 Ball, *Indeh*, 62.

135 Ball, *In the Days*, 11.

136 Ibid., 16.

137 Opler, *Life-Way*, 35.

138 Ball and Sánchez, "Women," 9.

139 Ball, *In the Days*, 11; Ball, *Indeh*, 62.

140 Ball, *In the Days*, 11; Ball, *Indeh*, 62.

141 Ball, *In the Days*, 11.

142 Ball, *Indeh*, 62.

143 John G. Bourke, *The Medicine Man of the Apache* (Glorieta, N. Mex.: Rio Grande Press, 1970), 473. First published in 1892 as a paper from the *Ninth Annual Report of the Bureau of Ethnology of the Smithsonian Institution for the Years 1887-88.*

144 Ball, *Indeh*, 61.

145 Ibid., 61-62.

146 Opler, *Life-Way*, 201.

147 Bourke, *Medicine Men*, 456.

148 Ibid.

149 Ibid.

150 Ibid., 457.

151 Ball, *In the Days*, 16.

152 Ibid., 87.

153 Ibid., 16.

154 Ibid., 15.

155 Ball and Sánchez, "Women," 10-11.

156 Opler, *Life-Way*, 214.

157 Ball, *In the Days*, 87.

158 Eve Ball, "The Fight for Ojo Caliente," *Frontier Times* 36 (Spring 1962), 40.

159 Ball, *Indeh*, 62; Ball and Sánchez, "Women," 10; Thrapp, *Victorio*, 3-4.

160 Opler, *Life-Way*, 345.

161 Katherine M. Weist, "Plains Indian Women: An Assessment," in *Anthropology on the Great Plains*, W. Raymond Wood and Margot Liberty, eds. (Lincoln: University of Nebraska Press, 1980), 262.

162 Niethammer, *Daughters*, 167.

163 Beverly Hungry Wolf, *The Ways of My Grandmothers* (New York: William Morrow and Co. Inc., 1980), 69.

164 Ibid.

165 Ibid., 70-71.

166 Ibid., 63.

167 Ibid.

168 Ibid., 65.

169 Ibid., 66.

170 Ibid.

171 Ibid., 67.

172 Niethammer, *Daughters*, 169.

173 Ibid., 170.

174 George Bird Grinnell, *The Cheyenne Indians: Their History and Ways of Life*, vol. 2 (New Haven: Yale University Press, 1923), 44-45.

175 Grinnell, *Cheyenne*, 44-45; George Bird Grinnell, *The Fighting Cheyennes* (Norman: University of Oklahoma Press, 1956), 336.

176 Niethammer, *Daughters*, 168.

177 Ibid.

178 John Philip Reid, *A Law of Blood: The Primitive Law of the Cherokee Nation* (New York: New York University Press, 1970), 187; Grace Steele Woodward, *The Cherokees* (Norman: University of Oklahoma Press, 1963), 48.

179 Reid, *Law*, 187.

180 Peggy R. Sanday, "Toward a Theory of the Status of Women," *American Anthropologist* 75 (October 1973), 1682.

181 Ibid., 1683.

182 Ibid.

BIBLIOGRAPHY

Primary Sources

Recollections and Published Papers

Ball, Eve. *Indeh: An Apache Odyssey*. Provo: Brigham Young University Press, 1980.

Ball, Eve, and James Kawaykla. *In the Days of Victorio: Recollections of a Warm Springs Apache*. Tucson: University of Arizona Press, 1970.

Betzinez, James, with Wilbur Sturtevant Nye. *I Fought With Geronimo*. Harrisburg, Pa.: The Stackpole Co., 1959.

Bourke, John G. *The Medicine Men of the Apache*. Glorieta, N. Mex.: The Rio Grande Press, Inc., 1970. (First published in 1892 as a paper from the *Ninth Annual Report of the Bureau of Ethnology of the Smithsonian Institution for the Years 1887-88.*)

Cremony, John C. *Life Among the Apaches*. Glorieta, N. Mex.: The Rio Grande Press, Inc., 1868; reprint edition, 1969.

Gatewood, Charles B. "The Surrender of Geronimo," in *The Papers of the Order of Indian Wars*. Fort Collins, Colo.: The Old Army Press, 1975.

Geronimo. *Geronimo's Story of His Life*, ed. S. M. Barrett. New York: Duffield and Co., 1915.

Griswold, Gillett, comp., "The Fort Sill Apaches: Their Vital Statistics, Tribunal Origins, Antecedents." Unpublished biographies at U.S. Army Field Artillery and Fort Sill Museum, Fort Sill, Okla., 1958-62.

Kappler, Charles J. *Indian Affairs, Laws and Treaties*. Washington, D.C.: General Printing Office, 1904.

Miles, Nelson A. *Personal Recollections and Observations of General Nelson A. Miles*. Introduction by Robert Utley. New York and Chicago, 1896; reprint edition, New York: DeCapo Press, 1969.

Documents

U.S. Congress. *Senate Executive Document 117*, 49th Cong., 2d sess., 1886.

U.S. Congress. Executive Documents, *Report of the Secretary of War*. 49th Cong., 2d sess., 1887. Washington, D.C.: Government Printing Office.
U.S. Congress. Executive Documents, *Report of the Secretary of War*. 50th Cong., 1st sess., 1889. Washington, D.C.: Government Printing Office.

Correspondence and Interviews

Ball, Eve. Interviews with author. Ruidoso, N. Mex., 10 and 24 June 1982.
Skinner, Woodward B. Letter to author, 7 February 1983.

Secondary Sources

Books

Debo, Angie. *Geronimo: The Man, His Time, His Place*. Norman: University of Oklahoma Press, 1976.
Delaney, Janice; Mary Jane Lupton; and Emily Toth. *The Curse: A Cultural History of Menstruation*. New York: E. P. Dutton and Co., Inc., 1976.
Goodwin, Greenville. *Social Organization of the Western Apache*. Chicago: University of Chicago Press, 1942.
Grinnell, George Bird. *The Cheyenne Indians: Their History and Ways of Life*, vol. 2. New Haven: Yale University Press, 1923.
_____. *The Fighting Cheyennes*. Norman: University of Oklahoma Press, 1956.
Haley, James L. *Apaches: A History and Culture Portrait*. Garden City, N.Y.: Doubleday and Co., Inc., 1981.
Hungry Wolf, Beverly. *The Ways of my Grandmothers*. New York: William Morrow and Co., Inc., 1980.
Mails, Thomas E. *The People Called Apache*. Englewood Cliffs, N.J.: Prentice Hall, 1974.
Melody, Michael E. *The Apaches: A Critical Bibliography*. Bloomington, Ind.: Indiana University Press, 1977.
Niethammer, Carolyn. *Daughters of the Earth: The Lives and Legends of American Indian Women*. New York: Macmillan Publishing Co., Inc., 1977.

Opler, Morris E. *An Apache Life-Way*. Chicago: University of Chicago Press, 1941.

Reid, John Phillip. *A Law of Blood: The Primitive Law of the Cherokee Nation*. New York: New York University Press, 1970.

Schroeder, Albert H. *Apache Indians: A Study of the Apache Indians*, pts. I, II, and III. New York and London: Garland Publishing, Inc., 1974.

Thrapp, Dan L. *Victorio and the Mimbres Apaches*. Norman: University of Oklahoma Press, 1974.

Woodward, Grace Steele. *The Cherokees*. Norman: University of Oklahoma Press, 1963.

Worcester, Donald. *The Apaches: Eagles of the Southwest*. Norman: University of Oklahoma Press, 1979.

Articles

Ball, Eve. "The Fight for Ojo Caliente." *Frontier Times*, 36 (Spring 1962): 40-46.

Ball, Eve and Lynda Sánchez. "Legendary Apache Women." *Frontier Times*, (October-November 1980): 8-12.

Gunnerson, James H. "Southern Athapaskan Archaeology." *The Handbook of North American Indians*, gen. ed. W. C. Sturtevant, vol. 9. Washington, D.C.: Smithsonian Institution, 1979, 162-69.

Sanday, Peggy R. "Toward a Theory of the Status of Women." *American Anthropologist*, 75 (October 1973), 1682-99.

Weist, Katherine M. "Plains Indian Women: An Assessment." *Anthropology on the Great Plains*, ed. W. Raymond Wood and Margot Liberty. Linclon: University of Nebraska Press, 1980, 260-65.

About the Author

Kimberly Beth Moore Buchanan, a native Texan, received her Bachelor of Arts and Master of Arts degrees in history and English from Texas Tech University in Lubbock.

She became interested in Indian history at an early age, inspired in part by lore and artifacts collected by her paternal grandfather. She has taught Texas history and English in public schools of Lubbock and Hobbs, N. Mex. Buchanan has presented research papers about women warriors at numerous symposiums and for classes in Texas and New Mexico. She is the author of an article about Eve Ball for *Historians of the American Frontier.*

Married to Dennis Buchanan, she has one daughter and lives in Hobbs.

Texas Western Press

*gratefully acknowledges
the following endowments:*

**The Mary Hanner Redford Memorial Fund
The Judge and Mrs. Robert E. Cunningham Fund
The Dr. C.L. Sonnichsen Southwestern Publication Fund**

*all of which make possible
this and other issues of*

Southwestern Studies